ALSO BY GUY A. ZONA

The House of the Heart Is Never Full

The Soul Would Have No Rainbow If the Eyes Had No Tears

Eyes That See Do Not Grow Old

Guy A. Zona

a touchstone book

published by Simon & Schuster

Even Withered Trees
Give Prosperity
to the Mountain

AND OTHER PROVERBS OF JAPAN

TOUCHSTONE
Rockefeller Center
1230 Avenue of the Americas
New York, NY 10020

Copyright © 1996 by Guy A. Zona

TOUCHSTONE and colophon are
registered trademarks of Simon & Schuster Inc.

Designed by Elina D. Nudelman
Manufactured in the United States of America
1 3 5 7 9 10 8 6 4 2

Library of Congress Cataloging-in-Publication Data
Zona, Guy A.
Even withered trees give prosperity to the mountain
and other proverbs of Japan / Guy A. Zona.
p.   cm.
1. Proverbs, Japanese—Translations into English. I Title.
PN6519.J3Z66 1996
398.9'956—dc20   96-25789
CIP
ISBN 0-684-82401-9

With loving pride to Rina, my firstborn granddaughter,
whose inner beauty and outer beauty are unmatched and unequaled

With much pride and love,
Grandpa

Introduction

$\mathcal{E}$ven before recorded history, the traditions and customs of Japan were handed down through what was referred to as the *story-telling clan*. Frequently, these traditions were explained and represented in plays at various festivals. As the years went on, the gists of these traditions were crystallized into short sayings, which were called *koto-waza* or *words that work*. Such sayings were the earliest Japanese proverbs.

When a wise saying, usually depicting caution or encouragement, was used often, it ultimately became proverbial and was handed down through the ages. This, I might add, is a form of evolution that can only please a wisdom-seeking world.

The teaching and perpetuation of their proverbs is still such a priority to the Japanese that their children even play a card game that teaches proverbs. This game has fifty cards that illustrate proverbs. As each player describes a proverb, the other players try to identify which proverb it is.

In early Japan, the common people, whether of town or country, knew well the bitter and sweet of life, making them keenly aware and observant of all facets of life. This is reflected quite vividly in their proverbs. *Seven falls, eight rises*, and *There is a piece of fortune in misfortune,* are good examples.

The Japanese are a polite, kind, observant, and moralistic people, who appreciate beauty—therein lies the bulk of the subject matter of Japanese proverbs. With the introduction of Buddhism and Confucianism into the culture of Japan, the essence of these doctrines quickly found its way into the proverbs of Japan. In many of the proverbs parallelism is frequently used. Such is the case in one of my favorite Japanese proverbs, *Things never change since the time of the gods; the flowing of water, and the way of love*. It is the use of word parallels that adds to the significance and deep meaning of many Japanese proverbs and creates memorable and uniquely vivid and picturesque images.

It is my sincerest wish that the reader of these beautiful proverbs of the Japanese people enjoy reading them as much as I have enjoyed researching, recording, and bringing them to you.

The silent person is often worth listening to.

✦

Be like the tree that covers with flowers the hand that shakes it.

✦

Gossip about another and their shadow will appear.

✦

A liar is the beginning of a thief.

✦

Though you may see another's back, you cannot see your own.

✦

Give food to the unloved hawk.

✦

If a water wheel exerts itself it has no time to get frozen.

Even dust, when accumulated, makes a mountain.

✦

The cow drinks water and it turns to milk, the snake drinks water and it turns to poison.

✦

Great trees are envied by the wind.

✦

Conscience is the living room of righteousness.

✦

Karma and shadows follow one everywhere.

✦

One wishes for nothing so much as that which one has seen from the outside.

"Once" is the beginning of all things.

✦

Misfortune can become a bridge to happiness.

✦

The road of time has no gatekeeper.

✦

Rocks are thrown only at fruit-bearing trees.

✦

What has been the fashion will come into fashion again.

✦

At the foot of the lighthouse, it is dark.

✦

Pinch yourself and know how others feel.

Laughter can seldom bring back what anger has driven away.

✦

Hearts are as unlike as faces.

✦

There is a piece of fortune in misfortune.

✦

Wounds afflicted by a sword are usually more easily healed than wounds afflicted by words.

✦

Where words are excessive, the quality is deficient.

✦

If you become lost, go back while you can see your way.

One who can talk well is also capable of lying well.

✦

When entering a new frontier, discover what is forbidden within it.

✦

Even the fortune-tellers do not know their own destiny.

✦

Where there is honor, there is no need of bolts.

✦

Proof is better than discussion.

✦

When the snow oppresses the branches, the pine tree nevertheless remains green.

The noble-minded love mountains; the wise delight in water.

✦

Even monkeys fall from trees.

✦

If one makes an offering, what does it matter whether it's persimmons or pears?

✦

To the ant, a few drops of rain are a flood.

✦

Rather than study an art, get to know it.

✦

A fog cannot be dispelled with a fan.

Small fish flock where big ones are.

✦

A falling leaf foretells the approach of autumn.

✦

Use the stick and save a fall.

✦

The reputation of a thousand years may be determined by the conduct of one hour.

✦

The string of one's sack of patience is generally tied with a slipknot.

✦

Curse your neighbor and dig two graves.

The person who confesses ignorance shows it once; those who try to conceal it show it many times.

✦

When the character of someone is not clear to you, look at that person's friends.

✦

The good walk on, whatever befalls.

✦

Though driven away, the dog of lust will reappear to tempt again.

✦

The man who makes the first bad move always loses the game.

✦

No dispute is possible without an adversary.

What one does, one becomes.

✦

All lust is grief.

✦

To employ another is to be employed.

✦

After a period of time, an evil becomes a necessity.

✦

The absent get farther off every day.

✦

Strike the face of a Buddha three times, and even his anger will be roused.

Too much courtesy is discourtesy.

✦

A watched tongue guarantees a carefree heart.

✦

The result of tolerance is contentment.

✦

It is difficult to be strong while not being rash.

✦

It is better to go to heaven in rags than to hell in embroidery.

✦

It's the tortoise that discounts the value of a pair of fast legs.

✦

The ignorant have their virtues, just as the wise have their faults.

Water does not flow out of an old river.

✦

Even the heart has boundaries.

✦

All married women are not wives; all married men are not husbands.

✦

The great parent is the one who does not lose its child's love.

✦

In the house where evil has piled up, evil remains behind for the descendants.

✦

There is no limit to looking upward.

When wrong passes on the road, right disappears.

✦

Even the wishes of an ant reach to heaven.

✦

The good deed is better than three days of fasting at a shrine.

✦

If that which is within is not right, it is useless to pray for that which is without.

✦

Give sail to ability.

✦

If you wish to climb to the top of the peaks that seem to pierce the sky, there is a way.

Waiting for luck is the same thing as waiting for death.

✦

A shallow river should be crossed as if it were deep.

✦

Don't make a Buddha without putting in a soul.

✦

In studying the old, we often learn the new.

✦

Wait! There will come nectar, like fair weather.

✦

Love lives in thatched cottages as well as in palaces.

✦

Good people are like the clouds, they receive only to give away.

What the wind brings, the wind carries away.

✦

When thou art in favor, they are ready to befriend thee.

✦

To teach others is to learn oneself.

✦

A face without a smile is like a lantern without a light.

✦

Thine own heart makes the world.

✦

The biggest room in the world is the room for improvement.

Gold is tested by fire; people are tested by gold.

✦

What is good is not necessarily beautiful.

✦

Kissing the baby touches the loving parent.

✦

Study others' advantages and they will become your own.

✦

Politeness is inward kindness outwardly expressed.

✦

When you forgive your enemies you weaken them.

An unkind statement, once let loose, often cannot be caught by four horses.

✦

What is difficult to understand, place before you; what is easy to understand, place behind you.

✦

By falling we learn to go safely.

✦

If you will it, it will not remain a fairy tale.

✦

Our greatest glory consists not in never falling, but in rising every time we fall.

✦

Adversity is the diamond dust heaven polishes its jewels with.

Even withered trees give prosperity to the mountain.

✦

Though tears fall they do not help to pay the debt.

✦

Virtue carries a lean purse.

✦

One can only stand others' pains for three years.

✦

After the swallowing, the scalding is quickly forgotten.

✦

Rubbish accumulates, mountains rise.

✦

It is not fear which makes cats meow but their confidence.

The world is dark an inch ahead.

✦

A true word is not beautiful and a beautiful word is not true.

✦

Yesterday is the "once" of today.

✦

Wisdom and virtue are like the two wheels of a cart.

✦

Not to speak is the flower of wisdom.

✦

Life is love and spouse.

✦

Not to know is to be a Buddha; not to see is paradise.

From poverty to profusion is a hard journey, but the way back is easy.

✦

Virtue is not knowing but doing.

✦

The loves of youth are as a cluster of silver buds, but the love of maturity is like unto golden flowers.

✦

There is always a wasp to sting a weeping face.

✦

Even in a village of eight there is generally at least one patriot to be found.

✦

Eating pears also cleans one's teeth.

One crane's voice is better than the chirping of a thousand sparrows.

✦

Keep misfortunes for three years, they may turn out to be useful.

✦

A good cat needs no excuse.

✦

Sunshine and rice may be found everywhere.

✦

Pleasure is the germ of sorrow.

✦

The poet, though not leaving his home, sees the whole world.

Fish and guests are wearisome on the third day.

✦

Send abroad the child you love most.

✦

Wisdom is a treasure for all people and for all time.

✦

If you dig a well, dig only in one place.

✦

Worms that bore holes in walls are silent.

✦

Even when three persons come together, there is a world of bitterness.

Where there is a channel, ships can navigate.

✦

Good generals have no children.

✦

Wine is the best broom for troubles.

✦

What you want to say today you can say tomorrow more elegantly.

✦

When a shadow falls across your path, look about with caution.

✦

Love reaches even to a crow on a roof.

It is the poor who give alms to the poor.

◆

Our own breast is the best wallet to carry our troubles in.

◆

To be beaten is to be victorious.

◆

Beauty is only one layer deep.

◆

In the hum of the market there is money, but under the cherry tree there is rest.

◆

Hearing is paradise, seeing is hell.

A lie has no legs, but scandalous wings.

✦

Lookers-on see eight pieces ahead of the players.

✦

There is no sword against kindness.

✦

A child is a shackle that ties its parents for the three worlds.

✦

Indolence is a powerful enemy.

✦

To save one Mon, one often loses a thousand.

Eventually, even a gushing spring can dry up.

✦

Bad beans, when put to sprout, grow only roots.

✦

Human beings are the soul of all things.

✦

The heart of a child of three years remains until he is sixty.

✦

There is more delight in hope than in enjoyment.

✦

A dog will remember three days' kindness for three years; a cat will forget three years' kindness in three days.

When fortune comes to a house the devil accompanies it to the door.

✦

Look the other way when the girl in the tea house smiles.

✦

When there is no truth in a maid, a round egg becomes square.

✦

An insect an inch long has half an inch of soul.

✦

Consult, even with your own knee.

✦

The old raven laughs at the blackness of the pig and knows nothing of his own ugliness.

When something falls in the hands of the painter or the lawyer, white becomes black.

✦

Poverty is more painful than four-hundred-and-four diseases.

✦

Thankless labor gains additional fatigue.

✦

The hand goes to the itching spot.

✦

After rain, the earth gets firm.

✦

Three persons in accord with each other can still have different opinions.

Reason and plasters will stick together.

✦

Recreation first, medicine next.

✦

It's the physician who breaks the rules of health.

✦

Those who die are poor.

✦

Day and night wait for no man.

✦

A borrowed axe is just the same as one's own.

✦

We can never see the sun rise by looking into the west.

Having waxed, wanes.

◆

A new servant works hard but twenty days.

◆

If I peddle salt it rains; if I peddle flour, the wind blows.

◆

It is not wise to stay long when the husband is not at home.

◆

A wind is as good as a thousand doses of medicine.

◆

Flowers will bloom on widows; maggots will be hatched on widowers.

The fly finds the diseased spot.

✦

Even the street dog has his lucky days.

✦

Even the fool has his art.

✦

Things have never changed since the time of the gods; the flowing of water, the way of love.

✦

A cat's best friend is its caution.

✦

A sorrow is an itching place that is made worse by scratching.

Be a head, though it be only the head of a potato.

✦

A knowledge of the sacred books is the beginning of wisdom.

✦

It is the melancholy face that gets stung by the bee.

✦

A tall tree is easily broken by the wind.

✦

After victory, tighten your helmet cord.

✦

A sea voyage of even an inch is an inch of hell.

✦

When stones will swim, the leaves will sink.

Children are poor men's treasures.

✦

Thine own heart makes the world.

✦

Where there is an advantage, there is also a disadvantage.

✦

The laden almond tree by the wayside is sure to be bitter.

✦

The back and the belly can't change places.

✦

Even a dead cherry tree can bring picturesqueness to a barren hill.

Cats do not like men with melancholy faces.

✦

Daylight will peep through even a very small hole.

✦

The dead have no tongue and tell no tales.

✦

Death is both larger than a mountain and smaller than a hair.

✦

It is the doctor that cures the sick when the sick do not die.

✦

There are some gods who abandon humans; they are the gods who know us.

Lust has no bottom.

◆

The second word makes the fray.

◆

If you want to get on in the world, first help others to get on.

◆

We live one generation; our names live to the end of all generations.

◆

Walls have ears, bottles have mouths.

◆

Early rising has three virtues and countless more rewards.

When praying to paradise don't make yourself a hell.

✦

Gossip lasts but seventy-five days; its effect is a thousand and five.

✦

Lookers-on have eight eyes each.

✦

It is a wise falcon that hides its claws.

✦

An evil deed remains with the evildoer.

✦

The eye is harder to please than the stomach.

What is an inch in our eyes is a foot in the eyes of our superiors.

✦

First the man takes a drink, then the drink takes a drink, then the drink takes the man.

✦

Seven falls, eight rises.

✦

Who associates with dogs learns to pant.

✦

When falsehoods take the road, the truth runs and hides.

✦

Accomplishments remain with oneself.

Beware of the returning arrow.

✦

Even one who is carrying a load of bad eggs fears going near a stone wall.

✦

Do not underestimate an enemy even though he looks small.

✦

If you throw cakes at people, they will throw cakes at you.

✦

Proclaim by your deeds who your ancestors are.

✦

The stupid leave the door an inch open; the lazy, three inches; and the fool, wide open.

The tiger leaves behind his skin; people leave their name.

✦

At least I have learned that the whirlpool of Diva is a calm, without wind or wave, compared to human life.

✦

A candle, by consuming itself, gives light to others.

✦

That which one would conceal easily comes to light.

✦

A mongrel dog barks bravely before his own gate.

✦

Scare away the flies from your own head.

The strong man can spin tops in the sand.

✦

Never follow the heels of sorrow; it may turn back.

✦

Our teeth often bite our own tongue.

✦

Excessive tenderness is followed by a hundredfold dislikes.

✦

An ulcer and a boil do not choose where to appear.

✦

Virtue is never alone; neighbors are certain to assemble around it.

Once bitten by a snake, one fears a rotten rope.

✦

A tree that bears fruit is known by its flowers.

✦

For traveling, a companion; for the world, kindness.

✦

The treasure that always circulates without an obstacle is cash.

✦

Seek shelter under a big tree.

✦

One might stop the flowing water, but the things that never return are the days and months.

Fortune will call at the smiling gate.

✦

The guests change, but the host remains the same.

✦

People are good when they are old; objects are good when they are new.

✦

He who sells a house gets the price of the nails.

✦

It is the hen that tells the cock to crow.

✦

Going downhill no one is old.

Fallen blossoms leave their perfume behind.

✦

Those in love take a harelip for a dimple.

✦

That which is eaten in the parents' house lasts three days.

✦

Old age is a medicine.

✦

A father's goodness is higher than the mountain; a mother's goodness is deeper than the sea.

✦

Brothers and sisters are the forerunners of strangers.

Ten people, ten colors.

✦

One meal without rice mars domestic happiness for a week.

✦

All good movements in social life begin at the top.

✦

A child brought up by its grandmother is five hundred yen cheaper.

✦

Everybody's voice is God's voice.

✦

He who never suffers persecution will never become a Buddha.

All religions start from Asia.

✦

Even hell's torments are measured by money.

✦

He who cannot look at others with a smiling face should not open a shop.

✦

The lotus springs from the mud.

✦

Clever preacher, short sermon.

✦

To rouse the village you must first rouse the priest.

Where profit is, loss is hidden nearby.

✦

The thoughts of one's heart are one's wealth.

✦

Too many boatmen carry the boat up the mountain.

✦

Good critic—bad worker.

✦

There is no door for the buying that will shut out the world of men.

✦

That which you would sell, deck with flowers.

If a few pennies do not go, many dollars will not come.

✦

An unskilled man's attempt is sure to be a failure.

✦

If you would be a dog, at least be the dog of a great house.

✦

Even a castle ten thousand feet high collapses from an anthill.

✦

The climbing of a height begins from the base.

✦

Ripe melons drop without plucking.

✦

A road of a thousand miles begins with one step.

To submit is to gain victory.

✦

He who would go a hundred miles should consider ninety-nine as halfway.

✦

We learn little from victory, much from defeat.

✦

Learn well, play well.

✦

Nothing is too hard for the arrow to pierce when the bow is drawn with full force.

✦

A good handwriter never loses his pen.

Drums sound as they are beaten.

✦

A day-old puppy fears not a tiger.

✦

The putting-off man sharpens his arrows when he sees the boar.

✦

Unpolished jewels do not shine.

✦

If the source of the stream is muddy, the whole course will be muddy.

✦

No standing in the world without stooping.

A year's opportunity depends on the spring, a day's on the dawn.

✦

Money is earless but it hears; legless, yet it runs.

✦

The rich man thinks of next year, the poor man of the present moment.

✦

If you look for the source of the River Yoshino, you will find it to be the drops of water beneath the moss and the drops of dew that fall from the reeds.

✦

Where there is comfort there is pain.

The rich man and the ashtray become dirtier as they heap up.

✦

Even when one sleeps on a thousand mats one only needs one.

✦

The very rich cannot remain very rich for more than three generations.

✦

Even with ten million "kokus" of rice one can only eat one's fill.

✦

A man without money is like a ship without sails.

✦

Getting money is like digging with a needle; spending it is like water soaking into sand.

When the oranges are golden, physicians' faces grow pale.

✦

In the gleam of gold even a fool looks wise.

✦

When food and clothing are present in plenty, good manners arise.

✦

Lend money to a city, but never to a man.

✦

Love is beyond reflection.

✦

The tongue is more to be feared than the sword.

A single arrow is easily broken, but not ten in a bundle.

✦

Unless you enter the tiger's den you cannot take the cubs.

✦

An ant hole may collapse an embankment.

✦

The crow that mimics a cormorant gets drowned.

✦

There are no national frontiers to learning.

✦

Courtesy is a business asset: a gain and never a loss.

✦

Pray to God, but hammer away.

We may buy gold too dear.

✦

There are no fish in clear water.

✦

Be the master of your heart but do not make it your master.

✦

When it is cold, there are no dirty clothes.

✦

When the floor is raised too much, the ceiling is too low.

✦

Where there is no fire, there is no smoke.

✦

The fish that is golden shall swim in the sun.

Our fate is bound about our necks.

✦

It is no use applying eye medicine from a two-story window.

✦

From the east, the root; from the west, the fruit.

✦

A roving dog runs against a stick.

✦

Doing nothing is doing ill.

✦

When old, consult with your children.

If you pray even to a sardine's head with faith, you will be granted what you wish.

✦

No branch is better than the root.

✦

Love flies with the red petticoat.

✦

Because there are fools, wise men look well.

✦

A lean dog shames its master.

✦

Game is cheaper in the market but sweeter in the field.

Through green spectacles the whole world is green.

✦

Even a welcome guest becomes a bore on the third day.

✦

Where there is light there is also a shadow.

✦

Where anyone listens, the ground becomes three inches lower.

✦

Open lips make cold teeth.

✦

When the cat mourns for the mouse, you need not take her too seriously.

Riches are a treasure for a lifetime.

✦

Without oars you cannot navigate.

✦

A slow fire, a smoldering fire; a wise man, a patient man.

✦

The gods have little power over people in their prime.

✦

Easily changed is a woman's heart.

✦

One can paint the fur of a tiger but not his joints.

Tomorrow blows the wind of tomorrow.

✦

Too much done is nothing done.

✦

Branches of willow trees are never broken by snow.

✦

No wind collects in the meshes of a net.

✦

At ten years a wonder child; at fifteen a talented youth; at twenty a common man.

✦

An interval of sleep is paradise.

No purse so fat as to buy back a lost appetite.

✦

Diseases enter by the mouth, calamity exits.

✦

Offensive-smelling people do not notice their own smell.

✦

The mouth is the front gate of all misfortune and the doorway to all evils.

✦

The lantern carrier should go ahead.

✦

The lamb drinks its milk kneeling.

Idlers have no spare time.

◆

Everybody has at least seven habits.

◆

One good word can warm three winter months.

◆

No person is without a fault; hesitate not to correct your faults.

◆

Moral people beget many children.

◆

There is nothing more dreadful than a fool, nothing more useless than foolishness.

To be strong in goodness is to be strong in wickedness.

✦

Scolded children fear not reproof.

✦

A person deprived of his liberty desires freedom.

✦

No one has ever suffered loss because of laughter.

✦

In a quarrel both parties are to blame.

✦

It is better to be ignorant than to be mistaken.

✦

Creditors have better memories than debtors.

As water lends itself to the shape of the vessel that contains it, so we are influenced by our good or bad friends.

✦

Against reason no sword will prevail.

✦

Where there is no antagonist you cannot quarrel.

✦

No company is better than bad company.

✦

Spouses and shoes are better when old.

✦

To pamper children is to desert them.

Women should associate with women.

✦

When passionately in love, we become stupid.

✦

There is no enemy like sickness; no love is equal to self-love; no power equal to moral merit.

✦

One dreams though one is awake.

✦

Who knows much, mistakes much.

✦

We look at others with our front eyes, but we see ourselves with those behind.

A drowning person will grasp at a straw.

✦

Pride goes before a fall.

✦

The outsider sees the most of the game.

✦

One hair of a maiden's head pulls harder than ten yokes of oxen.

✦

Though a beautiful woman remains silent, her looks cannot be hidden.

✦

Who spits toward the sky gets it back in their own face.

In accommodating others you accommodate yourself.

✦

Meeting is the beginning of parting.

✦

The best kind of acquaintance is acquaintance with each other's hearts.

✦

Hot love is soon cold.

✦

Nothing venture, nothing have.

✦

Not meeting makes one's loving heart grow stronger.

To endure what is unendurable is true endurance.

✦

Good talkers are the least doers.

✦

Choose a bride and piece-goods in the daytime.

✦

Where there is joy, there is sorrow.

✦

When drunk, we reveal our true instinct.

✦

There are no poor soldiers under a brave general.

✦

Superiority wins and inferiority loses.

Behind able people there are many able people.

✦

Little drops of water make the mighty ocean.

✦

Adversity is the foundation of virtue.

✦

By obeying we learn to command.

✦

Serious disasters come from small causes.

✦

What one dreads one must see.

✦

Virtue is not an orphan; it will always have a family around it.

Better remove the fish than drive away the cat.

✦

The cool head and warm feet are the cause of long life.

✦

It is because of muddy ponds that there are lotus blossoms.

✦

The "plain" must learn far more than those who are talented.

✦

When the bitters of adversity are exhausted, then come the sweets of happiness.

✦

If you are old, give advice; if you are young, take it.

Those who grasp at a small advantage incur a great loss.

✦

If you hate someone, let them live.

✦

They are never alone who are accompanied by noble thought.

✦

The wind and the cherry blossom can never be good friends.

✦

Where passion is high, reason is low.

✦

Wisdom and virtue are as inseparable as the moon and sky.

✦

Sake reveals one's true heart.

When you are among swans, you become a swan.

✦

To hear and see is good for the heart; when the heart is sweet it lives in the mouth.

✦

All colors are the same to a blind man.

✦

It's generally the most wicked who know the nearest path to the shrine.

✦

The butterfly, tempted by the flower, gets lured into the spider's web.

✦

Anger manages everything badly.

Lepers are always envious of those with only sores.

✦

The young crow shows its filial piety by feeding its parent in return.

✦

What is bought is cheaper than a gift.

✦

Wealth makes one's family prosper; virtue makes one respectable.

✦

It is as good as having one's bread buttered on both sides.

✦

Crafty eyes and loose lips were never modeled on the face of virtue.

If a post is smeared with the mud of the river bed, it will be of little use for its head aspiring to the heavens.

✦

The stone may hurt the dog, but not as much as the hand that threw it.

✦

Truth is revealed in excessive drinking.

✦

The sparrow flying in the rear of the hawk thinks the hawk is fleeing.

✦

Those discontented with their fate will accuse even the sun of partiality.

Among flowers, the cherry blossom; among men, the samurai.

✦

To overcome evil is worth three pieces of gold; to have no evil in the heart is worth five.

✦

Who sits in and who pulls the rickshaw are both alike.

✦

If one praises you a thousand will repeat the praise.

✦

The bosoms of the wise are the tombs of secrets.

✦

Who travels for love finds a thousand miles only one mile.

Cold tea and cold rice are bearable, but cold looks and cold words are unendurable.

✦

If a person be great even their dog will wear a proud look.

✦

If you wish to learn the highest truth you must begin with the alphabet.

✦

To the eye of a crow its young one has milk-white feathers.

✦

The pebble in the brook secretly thinks itself a precious stone.

✦

Even if you put a snake in a bamboo tube you cannot change its wriggling disposition.

Like ginger and cinnamon, we become more pungent with age.

✦

Our necessity is God's opportunity.

✦

Don't prophesy to someone who can see farther than you can.

✦

People know how to spend a million yen in marrying off their daughter but don't know how to spend a hundred thousand in bringing up their children.

✦

When you buy a vase cheap, look for the flaw; when someone offers favors, search for their purpose.

✦

As the country prospers, its martial strength gets weak.

We betray ourselves not in answering questions but in giving an account of ourselves.

✦

The heavens cannot support two suns, nor the earth two masters.

✦

The cat is not allowed to keep watch over milk.

✦

When unreasonableness pushes on, reason draws back.

✦

He who is strong in evil deeds is also strong in good.

✦

Success in love lies not in oneself, but in one's tact.

It is a moment's shame to ask, but a lifelong shame not to ask.

✦

He conquers a second time who controls himself in victory.

✦

Justice leans to the side where the purse pulls.

✦

The philanthropist has no enemy.

✦

Character rejoices in rest and peace, genius in motion and activity.

✦

It is easier to find two of the same face than two of the same mind.

We knock in jest and it is opened in earnest.

✦

Shave your mind instead of your head.

✦

Preach a sermon according to your listeners.

✦

Between two stools, one falls to the ground.

✦

The eyes speak as much as the mouth does.

✦

Self-confidence first, money second, and personal appearance third.

There is no king on the journey to the other world.

✦

The way that attracts most leads to ruin.

✦

The penniless traveler will sing in the presence of a robber.

✦

Though clad in rags, people can have a golden heart.

✦

Love me, love my dog.

✦

Be all things to all men.

✦

Patience pierces even the rock.

A thief takes naps in expectation of something.

✦

Habit, if not resisted, becomes necessity.

✦

If we had no faults, we should not take so much pleasure in noticing them in others.

✦

An untried friend is like an uncracked nut.

✦

Nothing is lost on a journey by stopping to pray or to feed your horse.

✦

The man who restrains his anger overcomes his greatest foe.

He who buys what he needs not, may have to sell what he needs.

✦

To preserve a friend three things are required: to honor him present, praise him absent, and assist him in his necessities.

✦

In plenty, think of want; in want, do not presume on plenty.

✦

Treason is never successful, for when it is successful, men dare to call it treason.

✦

Better be the head of an ass than the tail of a horse.

✦

Little brooks make great rivers.

A paradise on hearsay, a hell at sight.

✦

Be brave to ask so as to learn.

✦

Who is childless knows not love.

✦

In love and war, measures are not chosen.

✦

Time flies like an arrow and time lost never returns.

✦

Repentance never comes before the sin.

✦

The mind can make a heaven of hell, a hell of heaven.

Adversity is the parent of virtue.

✦

A false friend has honey in his mouth, gall in his heart.

✦

If one's mouth is shut, no quarrel arises.

✦

Loyal men appear when a country is in disorder.

✦

Most are atheists only in fair weather.

✦

One coward makes ten.

✦

One brings misfortune upon oneself by searching too closely.

The conquered are in the wrong.

✦

Such seed as is sown, such harvest shall be found.

✦

Love understands love, it needs no talk.

✦

Blossoms are the pledge of fruit.

✦

The perfection of art is to conceal art.

✦

A man is valued according to his own estimate of himself.

✦

Smooth words make smooth ways.

The sparrow near the schoolhouse sings the primer.

✦

One always returns to one's first love.

✦

Where might is master, justice is only a servant.

✦

A little knowledge is often a dangerous thing.

✦

Of nothing comes nothing.

✦

To live long is to outlive much.

Butter will not melt in the mouth of those with the look of indifference.

✦

Parental influence lasts forever.

✦

There is nothing completely certain under the sun.

✦

Pleasure is the source of pain; pain is the source of pleasure.

✦

Many words, little sense.

✦

Whom the gods love die young.

One today is worth two tomorrows.

✦

Idle people have the least leisure.

✦

He who is guilty believes that all men speak ill of him.

✦

An early rising has seven gains.

✦

An evil act runs a thousand miles.

✦

Beauty and folly are often companions.

✦

Have a lunch prepared from the previous evening.

Getting a thousand good soldiers is easy; getting one good general is hard.

✦

A hero is only known in time of misfortune.

✦

Fools and scissors require careful handling.

✦

Over the greatest beauty hangs the greatest woe.

✦

Today must borrow nothing of tomorrow.

✦

In peace, do not forget war.

Who would rule must hear and be deaf, see and be blind.

✦

The warrior lives an honorable life even in poverty.

✦

Sorrow loves the society of sorrow.

✦

Silent men, like still water, are deep and dangerous.

✦

All that is ancient is beautiful; all that is wise is rich.

✦

The good man is the only one who does not know what is amiss at home.

From short clandestine pleasures often comes long painful repentance.

✦

The pen has superior power to the sword, for it is the tool of the learned.

✦

Two birds of prey do not keep each other company.

✦

He who understands a hero is a hero himself.

✦

The humble cannot ever know the ambitions of the great.

✦

A bashful dog never fattens.

A little bait catches a big fish.

✦

Fifty paces or a hundred paces are the same.

✦

As water afar does not extinguish a fire at hand, neither can those absent aid you.

✦

In time of prosperity, friends will be plenty; in time of adversity, not one in twenty.

✦

Lost happiness never returns.

✦

Acquire new knowledge by inquiring of the old.

One cannot get two good things at a time.

✦

Art holds fast when all else is lost.

✦

A fool's wit comes after the event.

✦

Silence is the virtue of a fool.

✦

Believe only half you hear of a man's wealth and goodness.

✦

Wake not the sleeping lion.

✦

Good and quickly seldom meet.

Brevity is the soul of wit.

✦

Hunger is the best sauce.

✦

Who goes a-borrowing, goes a-sorrowing.

✦

We learn to be wise by the folly of others.

✦

The burden is light on the shoulders of another.

✦

The tastes of ten different people differ in ten separate preferences.

One can see a speck in another's eye but not the beam in one's own.

◆

Tell me the company you keep and I'll tell you what you are.

◆

Curses, like chickens, come home to roost.

◆

Humans are mortal, fame is immortal.

◆

It is not by a man's looks that his character is known.

◆

Rely not on tomorrow but rather what is at hand today.

Parental light is worth seven lights.

✦

Flowers that bloom in the morning will wither by noon.

✦

If you grasp it tightly, it breaks; if you loosen it, it flies away.

✦

The gods sit on the brow of the just.

✦

The sinner is never beautiful.

✦

Keep your shop well and your shop will keep you well.

✦

Years know more than books.

A gentle hand may lead the elephant with a hair.

✦

Truth can come out of jest.

✦

A person who boasts of his own wisdom is always considered a fool.

✦

Snakes follow the ways of snakes.

✦

A fox is not caught twice in the same snare.

✦

The future is a sealed book.

The poor eat little, but are at ease.

✦

The many must labor for the one.

✦

The more haste, the less speed.

✦

Perseverance brings success.

✦

Never deliver a command by listening to one side only.

✦

One beats the bushes and another catches the birds.

✦

The scraping hen gains; the crouching hen lacks.

He that is in hell knows not what heaven is.

✦

While there is life, there is hope.

✦

The wheel of fortune is forever in motion.

✦

Swift and fair is heaven's retribution.

✦

A cause is requited with an effect.

✦

God never sends mouths but He sends meat.

✦

The first hour of the morning is the key of the day.

If the sky falls, we shall catch larks.

✦

Better one eyewitness than two hearsay witnesses.

✦

The law is no respecter of persons.

✦

If you don't hear the story clearly, don't carry it off with you under your arm.

✦

Little is spent with difficulty, much with ease.

✦

Impossibility is the only good reason.

Take rather too little than too much.

✦

A bridled tongue is a guarantee of a carefree heart.

✦

Often truth has come out of falsehood.

✦

Eggplants never grow on cucumber vines.

✦

Demons live in front of Buddhist temples.

✦

Heaven has no mouth so it expresses itself through those of men.

If you lack satisfaction you cannot be deemed rich.

✦

Fortunate are they who know how to be satisfied.

✦

Old men for counsel, young men for war.

✦

They who touch pitch defile themselves.

✦

God dwells on an honest man's head.

✦

Sake is the precious duster of sorrows.

✦

Of the thirty-six devices, it is the best to take flight.

A monkey remains a monkey though dressed in silk.

✦

The tongue breeds the greater danger than the sword.

✦

Life is subject to decay; those who meet are bound to part.

✦

There is nothing that cannot be achieved with firm determination.

✦

Praise teachers while they are present, subordinates when their work is done, and friends when absent.

✦

Who finds comfort in the words of flatterers rather than friends is as preferring bones to flesh.

Cherish not that which is aloof more than what is near.

◆

Even though it pleases your sight, covet it not.

◆

Ten yen are within hand's reach, but twenty are too far removed.

◆

Don't prefer the picturesque grotto to your own dwelling.

◆

Don't undermine others with your tongue nor hurt them with your glances.

◆

If you must clear yourself, do it so as to make full light.

Affliction is the touchstone of friendship.

✦

Don't love wind more than water.

✦

Do not long for more than your share.

✦

If there is a question, there is also an answer.

✦

Talk with the priest and you will find you have sinned enough to die a thousand times.

✦

The sun does not feel wrath at a firefly.

Teach the small and the lowly gently; the needle with a small eye should be threaded slowly.

✦

Having killed the buffalo for food, don't begrudge the seasoning and spices.

✦

Ten mouths asserting are not worth one eye seeing, nor are ten eyes seeing equal to a single hand feeling.

✦

Three things on the earth are accounted precious: knowledge, grain, and friendship.

✦

Three-tenths according to abilities, seven-tenths according to custom.

Go quickly and return quickly, for there are yet many roads to travel.

✦

The more you know, the more luck you have.

✦

Silver hoarded is only worth copper.

✦

Act as if you were watching over an infant.

✦

One word spoken appropriately may last a lifetime.

✦

Thunder without rain is like words without deeds.

Human life is like a revolving lantern.

✦

One is as easily hurt by a bad-tempered man as by kicking a sharp-cornered stone.

✦

Poison is controlled with poison.

✦

When you open the mouth, open also the eyes.

✦

At first meeting, a friend; at second meeting, a brother.

✦

Each of us has in our hearts a lion that sleeps.

Obsession is like standing behind a wall.

✦

The wife makes herself known at the cradle.

✦

There are false truths just as there are true lies.

✦

The result of toleration is pleasure.

✦

Of whom we speak, theirs is the shadow.

✦

A friend looks at the head, an enemy at the feet.

While the devil is away, let us wash our clothes.

✦

It is the nail that sticks out that is struck.

✦

Looking up, we should not be ashamed at the presence of heaven, nor looking down should we be ashamed at the presence of earth.

✦

Those who are nearer your hearts are those who are farthest from you.

✦

An open mouth cannot be shut with surprise.

When the frog flies into a passion, the pond knows nothing about it.

✦

Love knows no enemy.

✦

Kindness is not for others' sake but for oneself.

✦

He who gives to the poor, lends to the Lord.

✦

Regret magnifies the loss.

✦

Keep not two tongues in one mouth.

Better to be a crystal and to be broken, than to be a tile upon the housetop.

✦

To teach is to learn.

✦

Never rely on the glory of the morning or on the smile of your mother-in-law.

✦

Man's life is destined by providence, but his luck is dependent on himself.

✦

One false report sets ten thousand people to believe it.

A loyal minister, if faced with death, will not change his countenance; a virtuous woman, if faced with danger, will not lose her smile.

✦

Almighty heaven is not indifferent to those whose hearts are earnest.

✦

A family in poverty thinks of a virtuous wife; a nation in turmoil thinks of a great general.

✦

Planning is in the power of man; executing is in the hands of heaven.

✦

Requite evil with kindness.

They are not brave who will not act according to justice.

✦

Man has a thousand schemes; heaven has but one.

✦

A man without determination is but an untempered sword.

✦

The old forget, the young don't know.

✦

Learning is like rowing upstream; not to advance is to drop back.

✦

Riches adorn the dwelling; virtue adorns the person.

Do not think any vice trivial, and so practice it; do not think any virtue trivial, and so neglect it.

◆

An inch of time on the sundial is worth more than a foot of jade.

◆

To go yourself is better than to send others; to do it yourself is better than to call upon others.

◆

Slander cannot make a good man bad; when the water recedes the stone is still there.

◆

The tongue is like a sharp knife; it kills without drawing blood.

Men are crushed to death under the tongue.

✦

His mouth is honey, his heart a sword.